贝贝熊系列丛书
The Berenstain Bears'

FUNNY VALENTINE
意外的情人节

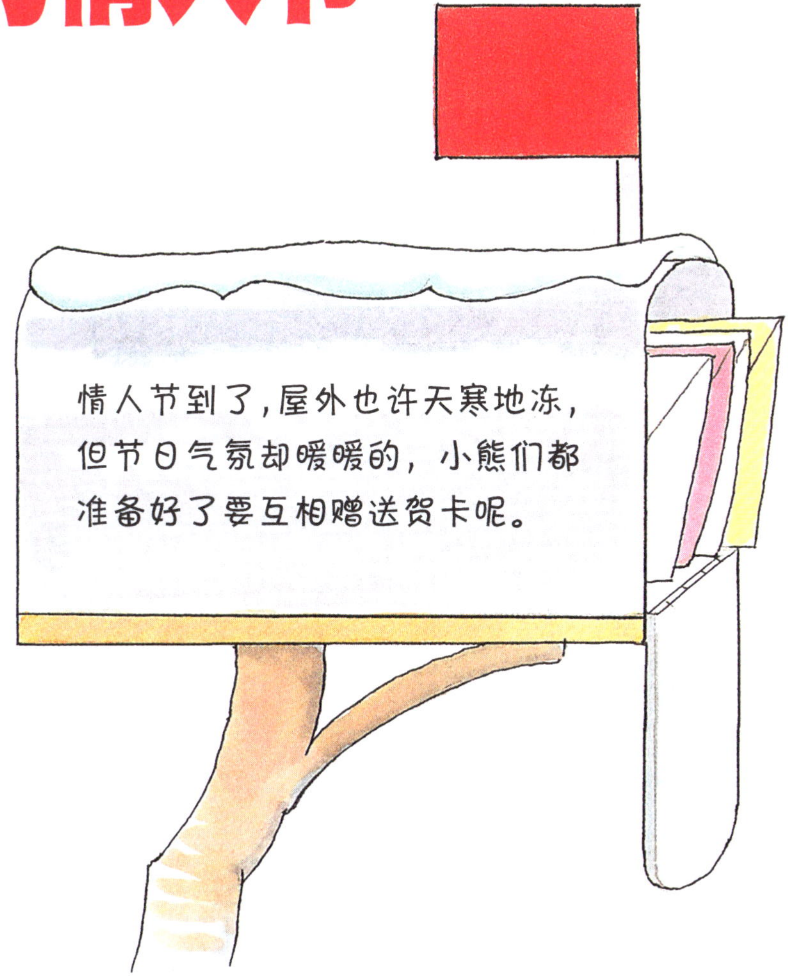

第一时间的启蒙书

你会属于
我吗？
你是我
爱你

贝贝熊系列丛书

The Berenstain Bears'

FUNNY VALENTINE

意外的情人节

（美）斯坦·博丹　简·博丹　绘著

Stan & Jan Berenstain

胥天　译

父母和孩子一起阅读

家长和子女共同成长

新疆青少年出版社

课间休息的时候，小熊妹妹和伙伴们正在玩跳绳。她们都喜欢跳绳，而且现在是二月，跳绳还可以让身体暖和起来。小熊妹妹和丽兹摇绳，艾米在跳绳。

“啊——哦！”丽兹说，“有一个男生从男生那边的操场过来了，你们猜他是谁。”

在熊王国学校里，并没有规定操场要分成男生专用和女生专用两部分，但男生们总是待在操场的一边，而女生们待在另一边。

“噢！最好是赫比！”小熊妹妹心想。小熊妹妹喜欢赫比，大家都知道——也许只有赫比不知道。

“是赫比吗？”小熊妹妹问，却不好意思转头去看。

“不是，”丽兹说，“是比利。”

“噢，不会吧！为什么是那个讨厌的比利呢？”小熊妹妹一边说，一边把绳子摇得越来越快。

“嘿，慢点儿！”艾米说。
“嗨，小熊妹妹！”比利打招呼说。

“别和我说‘嗨’，”小熊妹妹说，“而且你最好别像昨天那样拿着条虫子，或者像前天那样拿着只死老鼠！”

“没有虫子，也没有死老鼠，”比利说，“只有我自己！”说完，他就开始和艾米一起跳绳，却不小心被绳子缠住了。

几个人摔做了一团。

“干什么啊？你……！”小熊妹妹一把扯掉绳子，去追比利。小熊妹妹跑得很快，但是比利跑得更快，总是把她落下一小截儿。

“噢，为什么赫比不来帮我出气呢？”小熊妹妹一边想，一边把比利追得绕着操场跑了一圈又一圈。

赫比正忙着玩拳球，根本没顾得上朝这边看一眼。

这时候上课铃响了，大家都回到了教室。

“同学们，”珍妮老师说，“我猜大家都知道情人节就要到了。我们要举办一场情人节派对，有潘趣酒和小点心，大家还要互相赠送情人节贺卡。”

“太棒了！”全班同学都欢呼起来。

“哦，是吗？”小熊妹妹小声嘟囔着，“如果她觉得我会给那个可恶的讨厌鬼比利送情人节贺卡，那她可想错了。”不过小熊妹妹又想：“赫比会送给我什么样子的贺卡呢？”

直到吃晚饭的时候，小熊妹妹还在想这件事。这时，电话铃响了。

“可能是找你的，小熊哥哥，”熊爸爸说，“还是你去接吧。”

“没错，”小熊妹妹说，“也许是你的哪个女朋友。”

“你闭嘴！”小熊哥哥一边过去接电话一边说。

“我希望你不要再那样取笑你哥哥了。”熊妈妈说。

“嗯，”小熊哥哥刚一回来，小熊妹妹就问，“是你的哪个女朋友呢，邦尼、吉尔还是亚莱克西斯？”

“是邦尼，如果你非要知道的话，”小熊哥哥说，“她打电话来是问数学作业的。”

“啊哈，”小熊妹妹说，“那可不是她打电话来的真正原因。真正的原因是，情人节就快到了，她想确定你是不是会送她一张情意绵绵的贺卡和无数个吻。”

“你闭嘴！”小熊哥哥大喊道，“妈妈，如果她再不停下，我就——”

偏偏这时电话铃又响了。

“这次也许是吉尔。”小熊妹妹趁哥哥去接电话的时候说。

“亲爱的，”熊妈妈说，“你哥哥有几个朋友是女孩子，这没什么不对。情人节也没什么可大惊小怪的。”

“你妈妈说得对，”熊爸爸说，“再说，我好像记得珍妮老师每年都会举办一场情人节派对，我敢打赌你自己也会收到一大堆情人节贺卡的。”

“没错，”小熊妹妹说，“但那是因为我们必须这样做——珍妮老师是这样规定的。”

是这样的。小熊妹妹的班里有二十四个孩子，每个孩子都要给所有同学送一张情人节贺卡。价格不用太贵，而且如果你愿意，还可以亲手做。小熊妹妹想，她也许会做一张送给那个可恶的坏蛋比利——她开始考虑该在上面写些什么了。

“你在想什么？”熊妈妈问。

“呃——”小熊妹妹回答说，“我只是在想要送什么样的情人节贺卡给比利。”

“比利是一个和你特别亲密的朋友吗？”熊妈妈问。

“特别亲密的朋友？”小熊妹妹瞪着眼睛说，“朋友会在你跳绳的时候把你撞倒吗？朋友会拿着一只死老鼠追你吗？朋友会在你的饭盒里放一只会跳出来的癞蛤蟆吗？”

“我想不会，”熊妈妈说，“可是——”

“没有什么可是，妈妈，”小熊妹妹抢过话来说，“那个比利是个坏蛋讨厌鬼。如果他再来烦我……”

“为什么不叫你的男朋友赫比来阻止他呢？”已经回到座位上的小熊哥哥说。

“男朋友？男朋友？”小熊妹妹大喊道，“收回那句话！”

“所有人都知道小熊妹妹被赫比迷住了。”小熊哥哥说。

“妈妈，让他收回那句话！”小熊妹妹大叫起来，“我和赫比几乎连话都没说过！这里哥哥才是大众情人。”

“够了！”熊爸爸说，“情人节应该是充满乐趣的，而不是一场大嗓门比赛。”

“哼，如果哥哥停下我就停。”小熊妹妹气鼓鼓地说。

“那如果妹妹停下我就停。”小熊哥哥也赌气说。

熊爸爸把手指放在嘴唇前，他们两个才都停了下来。

小熊妹妹不用特意为比利做贺卡了，她在一家贺卡店里找到了一张非常适合他的。

卡片上画着一个科学怪熊似的怪物，面目可憎，脖子两侧各拧着一颗螺丝。

卡片上写着：

怪物可以是
奇形怪状的。
但要说到最吓人，
那就非你莫属了。

小熊妹妹在上面的署名是："猜猜我是谁。"她都等不及要看比利在派对上打开贺卡时的表情了。

然而，当比利打开贺卡时，小熊妹妹却忘了看，因为在她收到的贺卡当中，有一张让她惊叹不已。那张卡片上画满了爱心和鲜花，上面还写着：“你愿意做我的密友吗？”

“哇！”丽兹说，“这张肯定要花整整一美元。”

“署名是‘猜猜我是谁’，”小熊妹妹说，“你觉得会是谁送的呢？”

“嗯，我知道你希望是谁送的。”丽兹说。

“如果有人肯花整整一美元送给我一张漂亮的情人节贺卡，我肯定想知道是谁送的。赫比就在潘趣酒吧那儿，去问问他吧。”

小熊妹妹向酒吧那边走去，可是比利挡住了她的路。他手里拿着小熊妹妹送给他的情人节贺卡。

“我很乐意为你拿一点潘趣酒。”比利说。

“然后把它倒在我背上？”小熊妹妹说。

“不，不是那样的，”比利说，“我对以前做的那些事感到很抱歉。我真的不怪你送了这张贺卡给我，它很有趣。你喜欢我送给你的那张吗？”

“你送给我的？”小熊妹妹简直不敢相信，“这张贺卡是你送给我的？”

“是呀，”比利说，“我攒了好几个星期的零用钱才买下来的呢。”

小熊妹妹被弄糊涂了。她不知道该说些什么，于是只说了声：“谢谢。”

直到晚上她把比利的贺卡拿给妈妈看时，她还是没有弄明白。

“嗯，的确很漂亮。”熊妈妈说，“而且我也明白你的疑惑。这让我想起在我像你这么大的时候，有一个可恶的男生，就像比利一样。他真的很坏，做了许多可恶的事！有一次，他拿着一条蜈蚣追得我到处跑。”

“真恶心！”小熊妹妹说。

“这还不算最糟的呢，”熊妈妈接着说，“有一次，他把一只巨大的牛蛙放进了我的饭盒里。那东西跳出来的时候，把我吓了个半死。全班同学都被吓到了。这件事给我带来了很多麻烦！”

“那个讨厌的男生呢？”小熊妹妹问，“他自己没惹上麻烦吗？”

“哦，当然，那是经常的事！”熊妈妈说，“不过不久以后，他就改好了，后来又结了婚，养活了一家人，成为了一名好市民。”

“我认识他吗？”小熊妹妹问。

“认识，”熊妈妈说，“他就坐在那里，他就是你的爸爸。”小熊妹妹向爸爸望去，他的脸正埋在报纸里。

第二天课间休息时，比利来找小熊妹妹。
“我能问你件事吗？”他说。
“问吧。”小熊妹妹说。
“明天开会时，我们能坐在一起吗？”
“你不会带那些虫子或者癞蛤蟆吧？”
“不会，”比利说，“我保证。”
“那好吧。”小熊妹妹回答。

于是第二天开会时，比利和小熊妹妹坐在了一起。比利还给她带来一朵花—— 一朵雏菊。

小熊妹妹把赫比完全忘到脑后去了。

那天下午，小熊妹妹把比利送的雏菊轻轻地夹进了书里。

The Berenstain Bears'

FUNNY VALENTINE

It may be chilly outside when Valentine's Day comes, but little bears warm up and send cards to their chums.

1.Sister Bear and her friends were jumping rope during recess. They were jumping partly to keep warm because it was February and partly because they loved to jump rope. Sister and Lizzy were turning and Amy was jumping.

"Uh-oh!" said Lizzy. "There's a boy coming over from the boys' side of the playground, and guess who it is."

There wasn't any rule about a boys' side and a girls' side at Bear Country School. But the boys did sort of stay on one side of the playground and the girls on the other.

2.*Oh! I hope it's Herbie Cubbison!* thought Sister. Sister Bear liked Herbie, and everybody knew it— except maybe Herbie.

"Is it Herbie?" asked Sister, not wanting to look.

"No," said Lizzy. "It's Billy Grizzwold."

"Oh, no! Not that awful Billy Grizzwold!" said Sister, turning the rope faster and faster.

"Hey, slow down," said Amy.

"Hi, Sister!" said Billy.

3."Don't you 'hi' me," said Sister, "and you better not have a worm, like you did yesterday, or a dead mouse, like you did the day before!"

"No worm. No dead mouse," said Billy. "Just me!" And with that he began jumping with Amy and got tangled in the rope.

Down they all fell in a heap.

"Why, you . . . !" said Sister. She pulled the rope free and ran after Billy. Sister was a fast runner. But Billy was faster and kept just ahead of her.

4.*Oh, why doesn't Herbie Cubbison come to my rescue?* thought Sister as she chased Billy around and around the playground.

Herbie was too busy playing fistball even to notice.

Then the bell rang and they all went back to class.

5.“Well, class,” said Teacher Jane. “As I guess you all know, Valentine’s Day is coming. We’re going to have a valentine party with punch and cookies, and we’re all going to give valentines to each other.”

“Yippee!” cried the class.

“Oh, yeah?” said Sister under her breath. “If she thinks I’m going to send a valentine to that no-good, rotten Billy Grizzwold, she’s got another think coming.” But Sister had another think coming, too. She began to think about what kind of valentine Herbie Cubbison might send her.

6.She was still thinking about it that night at dinner when the phone rang.

“It’s probably for you, Brother,” said Papa. “So you might as well answer it.”

“That’s right,” said Sister. “It’s probably one of your sweethearts.”

“You cut that out!” said Brother as he went to answer the phone.

“I wish you wouldn’t tease your brother like that,” said Mama.

“Well,” said Sister when Brother returned, “which one of your sweethearts was it, Bonnie, Jill, or Alexis?”

“It was Bonnie, if you must know,” said Brother, “and she was calling about math homework.”

“Uh-huh,” said Sister. “But that’s not the real reason she was calling. The real reason is that Valentine’s Day is coming and she wants to make sure you send her an icky-sticky valentine with lots of kisses.”

“You cut that out!” shouted Brother. “Mama, if she doesn’t cut that out, I’m gonna—”

7.But the phone rang again.

“It’s probably Jill this time,” said Sister as Brother went to the phone.

“My dear,” said Mama, “there’s nothing wrong with Brother having friends who happen to be girls. And there’s nothing wrong with Valentine’s Day.”

“Your mama’s right,” said Papa. “And not only that, I seem to recall that Teacher Jane has a valentine party every year, and I bet you’re going to get a whole *bunch* of valentines yourself.”

“That’s right,” said Sister. “But that’s because we have to. Teacher Jane’s got a rule.”

8.It was true. There were twenty-four cubs in Sister’s class, and every cub had to send a valentine to every other cub. They didn’t have to be expensive and you could make them if you wanted to. Sister thought she might just make one for that no-good, rotten Billy Grizzwold. She began to think about what it might say.

“A penny for your thoughts,” said Mama.

“Er—uh,” said Sister, “I was just thinking of a valentine to send to Billy Grizzwold.”

9.“Is Billy a *special* friend of yours?” asked Mama.

“A special friend?” said Sister, her eyes flashing. “Does a friend knock you down when you’re jumping rope?

Does a friend chase after you with a dead mouse? Does a friend put a hop toad in your lunch box?"

"I suppose not," said Mama. "But—"

"There are no buts about it, Mama," continued Sister. "That Billy Grizzwold is a no-good nuisance and if he doesn't stop bothering me ..."

"Why don't you ask your boyfriend, Herbie Cubbison, to make him stop?" said Brother, who had come back to the table.

"Boyfriend? *Boyfriend?*" shouted Sister. "You take that back!"

"Everyone knows that Sister Bear has a huge crush on Herbie Cubbison."

"Mama, make him take that back!" cried Sister. "I've hardly ever said a word to Herbie Cubbison! Brother's the big valentine sweetheart around here."

10."That'll be quite enough!" said Papa. "Valentine's Day is supposed to be fun. It's not supposed to be a shouting match."

"Well, I'll stop if he'll stop," grumped Sister.

"And I'll stop if she'll stop," grouched Brother.

Papa put a finger to his lips and they both stopped.

Sister didn't have to make a special valentine for Billy Grizzwold. She found the perfect one for him at the card store.

It showed a scary-looking Frankenbear-type monster with a bolt on each side of his neck. It said:

Monsters come in every shape and size.

But when it comes to creepy, you take the prize!

She'd sign it, "Guess Who." She couldn't wait to see Billy's face when he opened it at the class Valentine's Day party.

11.But Sister forgot to watch when Billy opened her valentine because among the valentines she received was one that took her breath away. It was all hearts and flowers and inside it said, "Will you be my special friend?"

"Wow!" said Lizzy Bruin. "It must have cost a whole dollar!"

"It's signed, 'Guess Who'," said Sister. "Who do you suppose it's from?"

"Well, I know who you *hope* it's from," said Lizzy.

"If somebody sent *me* a beautiful valentine that cost a whole dollar, I'd sure want to know who it was from. There's Herbie over by the punch bowl. Go ask him."

Sister started for the punch bowl, but Billy Grizzwold blocked her way. He had the valentine Sister had sent him.

"I'll be glad to get you some punch," said Billy.

"And throw it down my back?" said Sister.

"No, nothing like that," said Billy. "I'm sorry about all the stuff I did. And I really don't blame you for sending me this. It's really pretty funny. How'd you like that valentine I sent you?"

"*You* sent me?" said Sister. *"You sent me this valentine?"*

"Yep," said Billy. "I saved up for weeks to get it."

Sister was confused. She didn't know what to say, so she just said, "Thanks."

12.She was still confused that evening when she showed Billy's valentine to Mama.

"Well, it certainly is beautiful," said Mama, "and I understand your puzzlement. It takes me back to when I was a cub your age. There was this awful boy, just like Billy Grizzwold. He was just awful. The things he did! One time he chased me with a thousand-legger."

"Yuck!" said Sister.

"And that wasn't the worst of it," continued Mama. "Once he put a giant bullfrog in my lunch box. It scared me half to death when it jumped out. It scared the whole class. It got me in a peck of trouble."

13. "How about that awful boy?" asked Sister. "Didn't he get in trouble?"

"Oh, yes. From time to time!" said Mama. "But after a while, he straightened out, got married, and raised a family. He became a solid citizen."

"Do I know him?" asked Sister.

"Yes," said Mama. "He's sitting right over there. It was your papa." Sister looked over at Papa, whose face was buried in the newspaper.

14.The next day, Billy Grizzwold came over to Sister at recess.

"Can I ask you something?" he said.

"I guess so," said Sister.

"Could we sit together at the assembly tomorrow?"

"You won't bring any worms or toads?"

"Nope," said Billy. "I promise."

"Okay," said Sister.

So the next day, Billy and Sister sat together at assembly. He brought her a flower. It was a daisy.

Sister forgot all about Herbie Cubbison.

15.And that afternoon, Sister pressed Billy's daisy in a book.